BEAUTIFUL

POETRY FOR WOMEN'S GROWTH & MOTHERHOOD'S JOURNEY

The First Three Collections

Juliette Proffitt
2022

BEAUTIFUL MESSY LIFE

For my children
Jack, Bailey, Erica, Ashleigh, Winter & River.
My love, life & youth. All for you.
Mum

***

For Ian
Always your girl.
Jay

Acknowledgements

With heartfelt and eternal gratitude to my late Aunt June, for spotting & encouraging the spark.

To my old music teacher, Mr Julian Taylor for having me repeat the words "I can and I will" in times of doubt.

To all my friends and cousin Nichola, for your everlasting support, love and encouragement. I am not lucky. I am blessed. Blessed to walk with you at this time in our lives. For the dark days, the good days and the better days we share. Thankyou for being exactly who you are and exactly what I need.

Thankyou to my childhood sweetheart Ian, for enabling me to be a full time, stay-at-home, home educating mother of six children. For giving the greatest gift a father can give - a mother who makes a home. A place that, whichever way they turn to look, they can find me there.

To my beautiful, precious little lambs. My children, who I wake for each day to show that women too have strength beyond measure. That dreamers can and do. Never give up trying to be the best you, that you can be.

To my father for your unconditional love. For being mine. For always being proud of me and making me feel like I am enough.

To my Joanie. For loving me so much.

Foreword

A poem can tell a story in fewer words, but with more emotion than a great novel could ever hope to do.

Poetry is written to be felt and to feel it you must hear it. To read a poem entirely to oneself "in your head" is to do it a great injustice. That is not what the poet intended.

They have poured a part of their very being into that prose. Liken it to a song that simply must be sung. Even when we're alone we can sing aloud from the heart. Poetry deserves this voice too.

Juliette Proffitt
(Revised October 2022)

AUTHORS NOTE

"Life, as I see it through my eyes."

This was how I began to write and it was therapeutic for me. However, it didn't take long to realise that whilst I felt lonely at times, I was never *alone* and that a great many of you who came across my "spilled ink" and poetry, also felt as I did. Then, instead of writing solely for myself, I began to write for you and my life changed.

My readers, followers and supporters. Many of you have become friends across the miles. I am humbled that you take so much from my simple words. Together through them we can smile when we need it, cry when we think we're spent and give each other hope and reassurance.

I will continue to write for you and for me...because together we are braver.

All my Love
Juliette

PART ONE

Dinner Pots & Lemon Drops

25 to 35

Winning

IT IS THEN

Your cries fill my heart

As they fill the room in which I lay.

The sweat of labour upon my brow.

You didn't ask to leave,

So why did I make you?

I hold out my hand,

A peace offering.

You grasp my finger,

It Is Then.

My need for you grows,

As quickly as your need for me,

Tiny hands smothered in lingering kisses.

Each finger, each line,

My tears fall upon.

I try, I do but

Time will not stop.

You smile at me,

It Is Then.

And so it passes,

Your innocent dark eyes,

entrusting me with your childhood.

I nourish, teach, shelter and love,

Smallest moments my proudest.

I wash away your sorrows,

And then cry for you.

You hug my waist,

It Is Then.

I watch you go,

My heart heavy, but

You will always be here.

Your smiles fill my rooms,

Your laughter trickles from my taps,

Your footsteps run across my landing,

Your elbows lean upon my table

And...

Your voice calls me, from my garden

Where you now sit, then rise.

You hold my hands,

It Is Then

April 2007

MOTHER

Most emotions have a place,

A time for them to show.

Kept in check, locked deep away,

With no place to go.

But never is there a time,

No day, no month or year.

When you should quickly wipe away,

The shedding of a tear.

For tears shed for your mother,

Are well deserved and just.

Never be embarrassed,

Cry fountains if you must.

She has cried a million,

For you since you were born.

Happy ones and sad ones,

So go ahead and mourn.

The only thing she'll do to hurt you,

Is to pass away.

And just before she does she'll cry,

For hurting you this way.

There's a time and there's a place,

For being brave and strong.

A time for thinking of those still here,

Time enough for getting on.

So while you both still have the strength,

Hold each other tight.

Even if you haven't done,

Since you were of knee height.

It doesn't matter if you cry,

She'll comfort you and scold.

Because she will be proud that,

She can still fulfil her role.

There comes a time in all our lives,

It's certain, this we know.

Our mothers need a well earned rest,

So kiss and let her go.

2009

ALWAYS

"Come in before you go to bed",
My Children apprehensively said,
Each and every single evening,
As their bedroom I was leaving.

"Always" came my quick reply,
"Always 'til the day I die,
Always if you ever need me,
Even if you cannot see me".

Lots of times I'd had enough,
Being mummy could be tough,
Through the day I'd often scold,
When they just would not be told.

And come their bedtime, I was done,

No more stories, no more fun,

Sometimes bedtimes were a chore,

Children always wanting more.

Heavy eyes and heavy legs,

Up the stairs, as slumber begs,

I would tiptoe to your bed,

Kiss you just as I had said.

My lambs, my youth, your tiny faces,

Unaware of how time races,

So precious you could never know,

How much I have loved you so.

And late at night all fast asleep,

I would lie awake and weep,

Knowing time would not stand still,

Knowing your bed you soon would fill.

Knowing that one day you would be gone,

No longer needing mummy's song,

Mummy's hand to stroke your head,

Or check you sleeping in your bed.

Knowing that I would probably stand,

In empty room with empty hand,

No little fingers soft to touch,

No lambs whom over I could look.

For now I lay across the hall,

Never asleep lest you should call,

Dreaming of my precious ones,

Forgiving them all their little wrongs.

And for now I'll try and think,

When they ask for "one more drink",

When I'm aching to the bone,

That one day, they will not come home.

And I will tell them as before,

As I head towards their door,

That I will be up very soon,

To check on them all in their room.

Always just a step behind,

There to catch you and remind,

That more than all the world I love you,

Always.

4 September 2010

SUNDAY BEST

For those who wear your Sunday Clothes,

Your fancy and expensive robes.

I want to tell you, indeed must share,

It matters not, what you wear.

My God loves me in my rags,

Without hats, high heels and fancy bags.

If I don't polish, brush and press,

My God doesn't love me less.

2014

PAVEMENTS

It's early evening down our street, I carry sweeties for a treat.

Home to my children and their dad, though all day they've drove me mad!

As I walk the short way home, there are many kids out on their own.

A pang of guilt I feel and doubt. Am I too harsh not to let mine out?

I do not try to keep them babes or allow them no taste of grown up ways.

But while other children hang about, mine are playing at our house.

Mine find games within the trees, there's a game to be had swinging through the leaves.

They find adventure in camping out, learning to carve and what fires about.

They make games out of tissue rolls, climbing frames and digging holes,

Under sheets and fancy dress, they play for hours and MAKE A MESS!

Sometimes I'd love to send them out, to join the kids that hang about.

That ride their bikes round aimlessly, out of my house not annoying me.

Some peace and quiet would be great, they could find fun beyond my gate.

But as I look more carefully, there is no game or fun to see.

These children they cause no harm. Use their manners behave with calm,

Mine are shouting racing round, laughing at some fun they've found.

Children playing "Let's Pretend", imaginations never end.

Very rarely found fed up, potions or perfumes in a cup.

No, I'm glad I keep mine in, It won't be long 'til I do give in,

But when they go they'll take their games and continue dancing in the rain.

Chasing rainbows, paddling in streams,

Older and capable but still having dreams.

I want for them friends and great escapes!

Not knocking around and swinging on gates.

To roam fields, get dirty and come back late

Be patient my loves, trudging pavements can wait!

2014

T-SHIRTS & JEANS

And I'm sitting there, shoulder covered in sick.

Piss on my hands, and I'm looking like shit.

My hair wonders what the hell a brush is,

And all I'm hearing is how you're full of it.

Never ever will you be one of those,

Mummies who seldom get to change their clothes.

T-shirt and jeans mummy you call the likes.

Well, that's what I wear, yes both morning and night.

'Cause sometimes it's easier to not get undressed.

Not to bother to wash, iron and press.

When your baby has had you up half of the night,

It's easier just not to put up a fight.

An expecting mum told me, (I felt like a jerk!)

As I asked what her plans were for returning to work.

That "Oh God yes!" Of course, she'd be back to her job,

"I won't be a non-person!" I felt like nob.

She said as she pointed to her swollen middle,

That "This one in here won't play me second fiddle".

And I'm sitting there looking at something like shit,

That lurk's on my jeans, as you're full of it.

'Cause, you don't know yet or you might have forgot,

That having small babies can take out a lot.

That my baby has slept every night in my bed.

I keep that hush, hush 'cause I know what they've said.

That it shouldn't be done, it might all end in tears.

But my baby, she needs me at night to quash fears.

She needs to suckle at least every hour,

How my breasts even make it, is beyond my power.

'Cause you know you eat breakfast and then you do lunch,

Maybe you sit with friends and you while away brunch,

Well, I ate my dinner last night at eight.

The only meal I got to have on a plate.

And I'm still sitting there, shoulder covered in sick,

Piss on my hands, and I'm looking like shit.

My other half wonders what sex even is.

And all I'm hearing is how you're full of it.

See that mum who leaves the house each morning before nine,

With her t-shirt and jeans, kids following in line.

Widest smile, kind voices, they all have their stuff.

You wouldn't believe that she's had enough.

On occasion, there are days when she's not doing well.

Maybe there are some things that she don't want to tell.

She could be alone, or afraid in the dark,

It might be too much, not a walk in the park.

There's one mum whose baby was born far too early,

Her Mister, he left before she had her girly.

And she's sat in Prem' for a million nights,

And she misses her toddler at home. It's not right!

She dresses in jeans that fall down off her arse,

She greets *everyone* with smiles, it must be a farce.

She's not long had a baby and you just don't see!

Your comments are quick and they hurt her and me.

This t-shirt you talk about covers a vest,

That shields my nakedness, conceals my breast.

So that people who have too much time on their hands,

Don't get offended by mammary glands.

But you wouldn't know about that yet, would you?

Or maybe you forgot how it affected you too.

When you found it hard to get a good start,

From feeding your baby close to your heart.

Maybe you forgot how food flicked at you feels,

As you desperately try to get bab to eat meals.

"A good strong routine," they say at the group,

Easier said than done when you're surrounded by poop.

It is hard to hear what your babes not done.

Sleeping through, weening, bleeding sucking their thumb!

Or struggling to just get them up, washed and dressed,

Let alone into bed just so that you can rest.

I have learnt how to pee in the middle of the night,

I have learnt how to breastfeed, and cook whilst I fight,

With my man as he also struggles to cope,

On two hours sleep and a Red Bull or Coke.

I know what it's like to hear the phone go,

At teatime, my God why don't in-laws just know?

That five o clock's Dinner Time, I scream and wail.

Don't call me to tell me WALMART have a sale!

So, I hoist my body up out of my bed,

Every morning the same, and just like you said.

I pull on my t-shirt, I'm not sure if it's clean,

I scratch off the carrot that's dried on my jeans.

I pull the brush through my need-of-dye hair,

I draw round my eyes to hide dark circles there.

And I sing "Wakey wakey, Mummy's little love",

She opens her big eyes as I gaze from above.

I smother her smile with kisses from mine,

Scoop her up and she's sick on that shoulder of mine.

I carry her downstairs attached without cover,

The love that I have for her can't match no other.

I plonk down in the chair still half awake,

I still can't believe that her I did make.

She strokes my skin as I make comfy my vest,

If there ever was one thing I did that was best.

It was to wear my t-shirt and jeans whilst in bed,

Wear, my t-shirt and jeans, whilst I fed,

Wear them I shall as I run round the park,

Not doddering on heels, in skirts up my arse.

I'll wear t-shirts and jeans as I clean the house,

Won't chastise grubby fingers as they grab at my blouse.

I'll read in them, climb, run, crawl and take care,

To remember that once upon a time I stood there.

When I get my chance to wear my fine clothes,

My glittering jewellery and beautiful robes.

When there occurs to me a worthy event,

That I wear my dress and think money well spent.

I won't forget how there were those days,

When my legs weren't privy to the summer suns rays,

To the mummies whose shoulders are still covered in sick,

When you feel all alone cause your man's being a dick.

We've *all* had our mister say "just take a look",

And we've lay there unable to move let alone touch.

You don't want to move you say "just let me be"!

And he grumbles and turns and you feel guilty.

And then, you and he, hear from inside their cot,

The gurgling and cooing of your precious lot.

You look at each other and it's worth every minute,

T-shirts and jeans. You're in it to win it.

2015

FRIEND

"Behold" began Old Man of Time,

"I'll let you journey but you are mine".

Many come, but fewer stay,

"Come on" calls Youth "I want to play"!

"Tarry a while" begs Mother of Trees,

"Set down your own roots and nurture your leaves".

Sorrow the Siren just shakes her head,

"There are no words, try Fate" she said.

And Fate just calls from behind the door,

"All for a reason, I've told you before"

Madam Fortune laughs wise and old,

I thought we were friends but "All glitter's not gold"

Yet I forge on, getting older and older,

Is that Grim with his hand on my shoulder?

Why does one feel lost and alone?

I long for a place to feel at home.

Then through the thicket, I see a light

Happy sweeps her step, lets me in for the night.

She has something to show me that I didn't see,

She fetches her looking glass, points it at me.

And there just behind me, (I feel my breath catch),

A cloaked figure enters and closes the latch.

The one who's been tiptoeing a few steps behind,

Hood down and you turn with a face that's so kind.

Relief fills my heart, how I wish I had known,

It was you all these years, definition of home.

Thank you for the journey, for just being there,

My friend, life is nothing without you to care.

2015

THAT I DID

Ah, my baby

My baby love

Mummy is so sorry

I didn't always have the time.

My lamb

My precious little lamb

Mummy loves you so

I wish we could sit forever together.

My life

Every single evening I race

Around doing chores so

That we might have some time.

Alas, by morning

I am tired all over again

You frustrated me and

I discovered yet another chore to be done.

I had to tell you

For this and that. Had to

Remind you not to do

A thousand things whilst I tried to get ahead.

So that

We could have a special evening

Or indeed that sacred morning

Maybe, maybe there will be time this afternoon.

And then

It is bedtime and I vow

That tomorrow we will have more time

Together just us two, time to just be.

But if ever

There is one thing

I will always make time for in my life

It is to tell you that I love you so that you will forever know.

That I did.

2015

GARDEN

Why is it the brilliant shades of Green

Look even more radiant after rainfall in the night?

Marvellous drops slide gleefully down my Flag leaves!

How is it that an ancient wall or basket hanging

A gigantic gnarled trunk, even a Terracotta Pot

Can create the most fascinating of Stories?

Who would have imagined emerald worlds

Under glass or even up high on the roof?

The wonder of a miniature breathing Earth in a bowl on the table!

Feathered, Wing-ed, Armed and Armoured!

Elusive beasts found nowhere else in the world

Hedge - Hog, Badger, Mole and Fairy would you believe?

Where else can one find peace

To rest in the arms of your young love?

To rest at the end of your days and reflect?

What better a place is there than a garden?

Glorious, seasonal, surprising us with life

Even when the winter ravages every corner

Green fingered retreat for all ages of women

Hiding place for many a man

Keeper of secrets, guardian of treasures!

Ah Yes! To look upon from behind my sink

Sit within as I grow weary

I can think of no better place, to lay my head.

2015

PLEASE DON'T FART IN THE MORNING

Please don't fart in the morning,

Don't fart in the dead of night too.

The baby's asleep, no not even a peep.

Please don't fart in the morning.

Must you always whine in the morning?

Must you always whine at night too?

No you can't wear a skirt, trousers don't show the dirt.

Must you always whine in the morning?

Why do I look shit in the morning?

Why do I look shit by night too?

Selfie status can't take it, fuck it I'll fake it!

Why do I look shit in the morning?

Don't call me before seven in the morning,

Don't call after seven at night too,

Try calling at five, and I'll eat you alive,

Don't call me before seven in the morning.

Oh, how I love weekend mornings,

Oh how I love weekend nights too.

Life ain't all that bad, though you all drive me mad!

Oh how I love weekend mornings.

2015

MARIONETTE MASTER

Beware, beware the puppeteer,

Seldom seen yet, always here.

They manipulate, stage and position,

Don't protest as they won't listen.

Their job is just to pull your strings,

And make you think all kinds of things.

Legend foretells they have gold shears,

For when they tire of repainting ears!

Without warning, quick as light!

The puppeteer swirls you to the right.

Silent. Smiling. SNIP! Relax.

Still hidden, while you all collapse.

Beware, beware the puppeteer,

Seldom seen yet, always here....

December 2015

PARTING

Tiny clothes laid on the floor.

Shoes shiny and new.

Holding each other very close.

Oh, how I will miss you.

Goodnight kiss and cheek stroked.

I gaze down at you.

My tiny little precious child.

Whatever will I do?

Morning comes much too soon.

You dress in your best.

I hold you tight against me.

In my big hand, yours is pressed.

I hand you over, smile at you.

Precious baby mine.

You smile back, then you are gone.

I hope that you'll be fine.

It's me you see, who can't accept,

That I must let you go.

I stand fixed and my heart breaks.

Right there, but you don't know.

I catch my breath and hold myself,

Then turn and rush away.

Tears are flowing freely now.

Why does it hurt this way?

At home the house is hollow.

No giggles, no chitter chat.

I worry about you all the day.

Keep busy with this and that.

And then it's over you are home.

Like we've never been apart.

School can have your mind, my light,

But I'll forever hold your heart.

September 2015

LISTEN

Oh, my love. My beautiful girl.

How I long to tell you.

How I long to make you understand.

How much I love you so.

When you were born I was the most happy.

The most I had ever been.

Alas, it's bittersweet.

You will be like me.

I want to raise you strong and proud.

Confident and decisive.

You will be so much more capable than me.

It is the way it was meant to be.

Oh, your Mummy is so tired.

I want to forewarn you of it all.

I wish I could make you "feel" the importance

Of my words. They are all I have.

You are such a beauty.

Be proud of yourself, your body, your mind.

So proud am I, of the woman you will become.

My love for you takes my breath away.

I must tell you things.

But I can't pen them.

There are too many.

So many, you won't listen in your youth.

But I have youth.

It's there in my soul.

My body is weary.

Mind beaten.

Aha! Look closer my lamb.

Through my tired eyes.

Past the wrinkled skin.

Into the windows of my heart.

I am there.

The girl dancing in the rain.

Skipping through the memories.

Skirts billowing in the wind.

I was like you.

I still am. Inside.

But the years,

They will creep up on you!

My love, my world,

Stay as lovely as you are.

Remember you can do it all your way.

All the time. Your way.

If it's wrong, make it right.

If it hurts, stop doing it.

Love, but be loved. Be mindful

Your tongue is a powerful thing.

Surround yourself with people

Who want to make you happy.

Let go of heavy things.

Carry only what you can't live without.

Make sacrifices for your children.

Always be a mother first.

Try to be a good wife

But not to the detriment of your being.

Finally, remember always how I love you.

Don't be cross with me when you realise it is harder than you thought.

I know, I understand. I don't know best,

But I know a lot.

Be kind, and you will always be beautiful.

I will walk with you, my love.

(For it is a long journey)

Forever embedded in your heart.

2015

PSST MAMA

Today you told me how you're not sure,

If it is alright.

To feel like crying when your child,

Tries to pick a fight.

Today you told me it was hard,

To try to keep your cool.

When your child misbehaved,

In front of friends from school.

Today you told me how it felt,

When you took something away.

When you sent your child to their room,

And there you made them stay.

Today you told me how that same child,

Screamed they didn't care.

They shoved past you and slammed their door,

And left you standing there.

Today you told me that sometimes,

You can sit and cry.

Wondering if it's your doing,

Just not knowing why.

Today they shouted, they hate you.

Today you thought things too.

Today might feel like every day.

Today, I felt it too.

Psst Mama! You are not alone,

My children do that too.

I also feel like I have failed,

A million times like you.

Psst Mama! Years I've waited,

For someone else to raise a hand.

To ask out loud for quiet support,

It's not going how you planned.

Psst Mama! I remember rocking,

My babe in my arms.

Vowing to do my job well,

To teach them right from wrong.

Psst Mama! I know how it hurts,

When they won't do as they're told.

To get to finish every day,

Feeling very old.

Mama's all around the world,

Look out and give more care.

Stop judging, competing, putting down,

Our worries we could share.

Years ago across the land,

Women did unite.

Helping each other raise families,

There both day and night.

Mama it is time for change,

Let's welcome back old ways.

Of keeping each other's spirits up,

Just like the olden days.

Today I turned a corner.

Today I helped you too.

Today we reached out and joined hands.

Together we'll muddle through.

2015

HE WANTS HIS MAM

Lies on the filthy blood encrusted earth

Eyes as wide as saucers

As the first bomb drops

He wants his Mam.

Runs like the clappers

Hunched shoulders like he thinks they'll protect his head

Silly Sod!

He wants his Mam.

Sheer terror trickles through his veins

Teeth clamped to prevent his lip from quivering

Be a Man!

He wants his Mam.

Throws a quick glance at the other "little boys"

Playing soldiers, "BANG, BANG!"

For your country

He wants his Mam.

Foul smells engulf the mad chaos

Men charge this way and that

Unhinged monsters of War

He wants his Mam.

Weapons clutched in white-knuckled fingers

Bits of lads strewn about

Honourable, "We Need You"!

He wants his Mam.

Glorious, Victorious, Brave

Bah! Babies, sons, husbands, fathers

LEST WE FORGET

He wants his Mam.

11 November 2015

FOREVER LOVE

I remember you.

The smiling, confident face in the frame, in the album.

The one that sometimes catches me by surprise when I least expect it.

Youthful, sure, sensual. We were one and the same.

Is it you or is it me?

I remember you.

How it was. In the photo booth. Stealing kisses behind the curtain.

Pretending we knew what we were doing.

Playing a dangerous game. Loving for lust. Lusting for love.

Was it you or was it me?

I remember you.

The strong, supple, youthful frame in the frame.

Tender, considerate, unselfish, fulfilling.

Making plans, starting out.

Was it you or was it me?

I remember you.

Blossoming, no blooming! Matured and capable.

That proud expression in the frame.

Ambitious, certain, harder with experience. Uncompromising.

Was it you or was it me?

I remember you.

Relentless, tired, short tempered. Fake smile, tell-tale stare.

Ah, look! One that gave you away.

The one just after the argument.

Was it you or was it me?

I remember you.

The finger on the lens behind the camera.

The feet next to the child on the floor.

The many with the heads missing. There are hundreds like that.

Was it you or was it me?

I remember you

The photo of you walking away, the "natural, unawares, picture from behind".

The saddest, most poignant one, in the box.

Us side by side, NOT holding hands.

How could that be you? How could it be me?

We used to love to fill the spaces.

In the album, in the frame, on the wall.

But wait! You have recognition in your eyes.

It doesn't matter who it was.

It's there. It's still there.

2015

NOT THE QUEEN'S SPEECH

Christmas be the most wonderful time of the year.

Be you Christian, Catholic, Mormon or Jewish.

Be you Muslim, Sikh, Hindu or Buddhist.

Scientologist, Tarot Reader, Tree Hugger, Numerologist.

Astrologist, Agnostic or Athiest.

It matters not. I don't give a hoot!

Share it with me.

Sit at my table this once.

Let us put our suspicions aside.

Let us talk about the wise men and how far they must have
travelled,

Let us talk about Babushka and how shit it was,

That she missed the babe.

Let us talk about the fact Mary's story makes

Her sound like a fallen woman and yet!

Joseph stood by her because of loyalty, devotion & love.

Religion. Good, bad or ugly.

Pipe down, sit down, be quiet and get over yourselves!

The reason behind the date on the calendar.

Take that story and tell it to someone else

Chuckle at its absurdity,

Look fondly at your friends and family,

The colours, the creeds and cultures.

Take that story and make it into something meaningful

For you.

Take stories from all around the world,

Create traditions.

Borrow snippets from each legend that passes your ears.

Pick out your most favourite parts.

Learn how to believe without cold hard proof that

As well as holiness there is magic!

Christmas can rightfully keep its name.

It can ring its bells and sing its songs,

And tell its stories for the whole world to hear

Because...

Christmas is not selfish.

Sod the racists, fascists and prejudice on social media,

Let them tut and draw sharp intakes of breath,

Through pursed lips as they hurry on by.

Jog on! My crowd have no time for the likes of them.

I took my daughter to see the mandir

And we marvelled over its beauty, I told her

"This Muslim house is like any other."

The old lady in the street grumbled

About the street being taken over for Diwali

And that we can't say Merry Christmas anymore.

Merry Christmas.

Merry Christmas.

Merry Christmas to you!

Don't talk such tripe, lady who should know better.

Lady who sets a bad example to my child as she stares on.

Lady who spouts about the youth of today,

The lack of respect to elders.

I respect those who respect others.

Shame on you. Here!

Borrow my glasses.

They will help you to see past the end of your own nose.

It is Christmas everyone. Joy to the world.

That's right! Joy to the world!

Those who practice faith tell their children

"God is love."

I say, tell it whatever way you like.

Christmas, like love, is more than a word.

It is a feeling.

And it's to be shared.

Come. Sit at my table this once.

Let us put our suspicions aside

And bring your God with you.

2015

SUNSHINE WHEN IT RAINS

Let's hold hands now, follow me.

I'll show you the way.

Safe and loved, never lost.

Just like yesterday.

I can hold that, please don't try.

Mind that you don't slip.

Let me tie your shoes and scarf.

Make light work of your zip.

Do you think you should go out tonight?

It's cold and dark out there.

I can take you, pick you up,

To show you that I care.

Look! I made your favourite tea.

Come on, just one more spoon.

I can read aloud or sing.

It's bedtime very soon.

Sleep and dream of happy times.

I won't be far away.

I'll always be right by your side.

I am here to stay.

Father, I do these things because,

You never caused me pain.

And I would do them every day,

Some sunshine when it rains.

So, let's hold hands now, follow me.

I'll show you the way.

Safe and loved, never lost.

Just like yesterday.

2015

CHRISTMAS PAST

There I sit, Little Girl

Fast asleep in the chair by the

Roaring fireplace. Waiting.

"Aha! I knew you'd be here!"

He chuckles as he tumbles

Into the room. "Every year the same."

"Yet, this year so melancholy,

Reminiscent, wistful. Where..."

He begs "..is the merriness"?

"Well now, precious child,

This year, something different.

Something that will last".

He draws his swag close,

On one knee. he searches.

Until "Got it!" But what?

"Christmas Past" he breathes.

And I don't understand,

But I close my eyes anyway.

Childhood & its decade of

Christmas times, wash

Across my angelic face.

And my cheeks glow with excitement.

Warmth, safety. Love.

A truly simple time, not a trial in sight.

My eyes flicker open as the memory

Roots itself firmly in my heart.

My visitor & warm fire long gone.

Still, the smile on my lips remains.

My thirty-four year old hands

Brush the Santa Dust from the arm of the chair.

December 2015

TALLY

And so the eve is upon us

The clock ticks a heavy "Tock"

A full calendar of promises silenced

Echoes of youth and laughter

Bounce around damp, fusty walls

Happy New Year!

December 31 2015

CLEAN SLATE

Morning breaks through curtains

Hands rub sore heads

Sporting sheepish grins

Clean shirts pulled on, fresh from the packet

The meal is dished

Conversations of new hope take turns around the table

Somewhere far away a giant fateful hand tips the sand glass

365 days.....GO!

January 1 2016

PART TWO

Minding The Muse

35 to 39

Losing

GREEN TEA & POETRY

Come closer now

What think you see?

Green tea cups and poetry

Lend your ear

Seat yourself

What seek you, from my bookshelf?

2016

ZEPHYR

I'm uneasy as she comes,

When I sit outside,

Wondering at life.

Whispering through the grass blades,

Gently, to "woo" you.

The "swish, swish" sound of her skirts.

Some delight in lying in the sun,

As she weaves,

Her way through the daisies.

You who doze beneath her kisses,

Know not that she teases the down on my arms,

And only ever breathes in my ears, a resounding "No".

2016

SPIRIT

He's on top of the hill,
Sat, sitting just he,
Old head held up high,
One hand on his knee.

He surveys the decent,
With the eye of a youth,
His steed of two wheels,
Near the moment of truth.

His wife wanted plant pots,
At back of the shed,
His rusty old steed,
He discovered instead.

"You're 80! Daft Bugger!"

His wife did implore,

"And it's all busted up,

You can't ride that no more!"

He clamped his lips tight,

His wife knew the look well,

He began work on the bike,

With its rusty old bell.

And now here he is,

At the top of the hill,

The school lads are hushed,

And they're all standing still.

The breeze is just perfect,

The sun beaming down,

He nods at his wife,

Winks "Look who can't now!"

A whisper escapes him,

"Ol' Gel keep me safe",

With a grin ear to ear,

The years fall away.

The wind whistles by him,

He rides straight and true,

Punches air at the bottom,

Victorious and new.

Nought in his life,

Could ever give childish joy,

Than riding his bike,

An old man, turned to boy.

May 2016

(Gel pronounced "G - ell" is an English reference to or term of endearment for a girl in some dialects.)

JUST A BOY

Just a boy, you were,

When our eyes first met.

Cheeky grin and moppy hair,

Cocky lad about town!

Your hair's a little greyer now,

And your cheeks are rough,

But your eyes!

They're still the same.

2016

TRUTH SEEKER

A lot can be found,

At the back of a stare.

Search for the truth,

You'll uncover it there.

Deep in the dark,

The Soul-Keeper resides.

Yes. It is He,

Who stares out through those eyes

2016

HARAMBE

The fools of the Tarot who thought,

Our Man-Brain so great that we allowed it,

To convince us to put a beast in a box.

I beg you to consider for once,

Just who it really should be.

Imprisoned in a cage.

Revised 2022

(First published 2016)

(Harambe was a western lowland gorilla who lived at the Cincinnati Zoo. In 2016, a three-year-old boy climbed into the gorilla enclosure where he was grabbed by Harambe. Fears for the boy's life resulted in a zoo worker shooting and killing Harambe. The incident caused much controversy and highlighted the danger of zoo animals near humans and the need for better standards of care).

TEASE

Her teeth grip a wooden peg

Arms ache above her head

Perspiring brow and underarm

Hair tied high, swings like a charm

He views her neck, slim and tender

Tangled in the sheet, her figure slender

She knows he looks on from his chair

Lazy dog days, sprawling there

A slow smile creeps across her lips

She bends gloriously as he sips

Stretching up like a cat

Backhands his lip, adjusts his cap

The grass ripples, breeze within the leaves

She's hot now, glowing brilliantly

Summer slumbers in hazy heat

Moves the basket at her feet

Empty now, it's on her hip

Near her "Watcher", breathing quick

Grin as wide to match his own

She tips his hat, then flees for home!

2016

UNBIDDEN

Unbidden

Come the voices in my head

They just let themselves in!

Cheeky Beggars

Competing for the space between my ears

They mean no harm

Mostly want to reminisce

"Please leave me still

The memories simply sadden me now."

2016

THERE ARE NO WORDS

I don't have all the words.

Sometimes,

There are none.

No right ones

In any case.

A tad worrisome,

In my position.

To find myself

Staring into your soul.

No comfort to offer.

And still!

Feelings are enough.

Words can get

in the way

Of all the "feeling".

They can spill out

All monotone and unnecessary.

Forcing you

To try to say that

You'll be alright before you believe it.

If there were some words

Some right ones, to take away the hurt,

I would not give them

To you freely.

I would hide them.

For those are better

Left unsaid.

Does the love you lost

Not deserve your tears?

Your broken heart?

No, I don't have all the words.

Sometimes,

There are none.

No right ones

In any case.

2016

NOTED

On the days that I failed you

Know that, I knew I did

You did not go unnoticed

Even as I held up my hand to halt your words

I heard your voice break

Saw your face crumple

As one, then another hot teardrop fell

On the days that I failed you

Know that, I knew I did

You did not go unnoticed

Even as I turned my cheek and dismissed you

I heard your heart stop singing

Saw your eyes beg me to tell you

Why I had gotten it all so wrong

On the days that I failed you

Know that, I knew I did

I hope you never noticed

My struggle, my inexperience, my heartache

I pray you never heard my silent

Cries to the night

Trying to figure it all out

On the days that I failed you

Know that, I knew I did

Know that I cared enough

To notice

2016

NOT SO THE BOY

Boys are not for pursuing,

Men & dreams make much better targets.

Not so the boy.

The boy should realise himself without you,

You'll discover you dislike the man.

And he will too.

Boys are not for pursuing.

You will make a neglectful man from the sweat of a tired boy.

No, you leave well alone.

Pretty, young girls,

Are good ingredients for lonely, tear stained faces.

The ones that go ignored now.

2016

EYES CLOSED

Tonight when we danced,

I fell deep into your eyes.

I felt you smile as you kissed my lips.

I like to keep my eyes closed.

I whispered to the glorious harvest moon

As we drove home, how special you make me feel.

The breeze from the open window played with my hair.

I like to keep my eyes closed.

We talked into the darkness,

And shared the secret sort of laughter,

Only those who are deeply in love feel.

I like to keep my eyes closed.

You last longer that way.

2016

CIRCLE

And so on it goes

Nobody knows

How many times I'll go around

This circle

That is you and me.

You just ahead

My hand outstretched.

Do you look back

Along the track

When I pause to dab my eyes?

Do you will me on?

Purposefully slow

I'll never know.

In recent times

Within my mind

A soft voice breathes "what if?"

And though I wake

I cannot shake

The uncomfortable feeling

Every ounce of my being

It takes to "Not Think".

For if I do allow it space

I can't be certain of its place.

And so on it goes

Nobody knows

How many times I'll go around

This circle

That is you and me.

You just ahead

My hand outstretched.

Sometimes the voice

Gives me no choice

Appears with image in tow

Aging and quivering

Begs me to listen.

Asks me to consider

This Old Man River

"What is, forward or backwards of a circle?"

Are you just out of reach or

Am I further from your grasp?

Dares me myself to ask.

Are you really running away or hoping to bump into me?

2016

LATE AUTUMN TREES

Will you remember,

Each year in November,

How I'd make you go for a drive?

To the late autumn trees,

With their red and gold leaves,

And I'd tell you to look as we quietly passed by.

Was the sentiment lost?

My words quickly forgot

Or did you feel it like me?

When I'm little and old,

Can we still search for gold?

And loves crimson embers, in the late autumn trees.

2016

PANDORA

Tired, am I of feeling misread

Wondering if I should

Or could

Or if you ever would.

Pandora just outside my head

Rattling the lock.

I have bought hours of lost sleep

With hot, steamy pennies shaped like tears

Just to keep her at bay

Staring at Orchid Blossom walls

I no longer care about

Fool enough to think myself a small triumph had.

Ha! That wide-eyed bitch

Just bent down and peered right through the keyhole instead.

Into a mind I never knew I had

Feelings I didn't

Notions that maybe

If I dared to think on it

The grass might taste sweeter elsewhere.

What change has become me?

Why does that crazed woman now begin rattling the lock?

Does she want to expose me for all to define?

Hope passes before her wanton gaze

Steady, slow enough to grasp but hiding her reflection well.

Not so pretty a face

Is the one that begs me to believe,

There is still something left, worth fighting for.

January 2017

SHAME

This place not for likes of me,

Capped justice, peace, equality.

Lost days of tea and empathy,

You cease, to empower me.

Revised 2022

(First published January 2017)

BED MATE

I think you think me very weak,

Dull without much brain.

If I could show you more of me,

I think you'd think again.

I like to hold my values close,

Know when I've made my bed.

By daylight, I forgive your words,

I sleep with them instead.

2017

NOT SO SHABBY

So, I stopped you,

In your tracks.

The slow and steady ones you tread,

In dilapidated shoes that should have been shelved years ago.

I made you nervous, yes?

Pricked your conscience?

Picked and plucked at that whisper of a fragile thread,

You thought you had tucked in as tightly as you tucked in your tongue.

It's OK.

Put your shoes back on.

Come now, don't be silly.

Stop hiding them, criss-crossed under your chair.

I do not concern myself with price tags.

My own glass slippers fell off some time past...

Alas, 'twas the Ruby ones that didn't fit.

It happens.

Ah, but I still dance!

To the same tune as you.

The same one that causes you to tap your toes.

I dance it barefoot.

2017

SELFISH

I think I'll take a little time
Just for me if you don't mind
You see I've not felt very well
And there's been no one to tell.

So I've felt a need to lie
Plastered smiles, steady eyes
I'm very tired now I think
And I haven't slept a wink.

I need no sympathy today
Violins don't need to play
I'm just going to hide a bit.
Away until I feel less shit.

It's time to nestle anyhow

The winters here, it's Yuletide now

I haven't strength sadly, this year

To write and send out cards I fear.

I can't make another date

If you're not booked then it's too late

I'll be fine with who I choose

To add some sparkle to my shoes.

So please don't judge me, let me be

I'll soon be back to me, you'll see

For now, just leave my door un-knocked

Unless you're Santa, it stays locked.

November 2017

JANUS

Dance, lovely girl!

Skip up and down the hallways.

Spin!

Audition for life.

Cast for lust.

Rehearse time and again for love.

Accept bad parts,

And play them fabulously, Darling.

Janus backstage, his smile in the past,

Eye on the future.

Offering another chance,

Another passage un-trodden,

To make good out of storms.

Take on this bright, new world,

Satin Slippered Dancer.

The Fool is ready to run away with you.

December 31 2017

SNOW PUDDLES

What could be greater, in grass colour of hay,

To float sticks in snow puddles melting away?

As sun kisses your hair and warms the spring day,

And you can stay long,

Learning "lore" and through play.

March 2018

SOULFUL TRUTH

Too often these days I find I'm frustrated

After the "chi-chuk" sound my phone makes

As it takes the selfie I hope will reveal the "soul" and purpose of my essence

Should anyone care to look into the darkness of my eyes.

I discard one after another photo

As each time I look, I see age and weariness

Where once would lie a freshness mixed with mystery

I do not feel fresh. My eyebags ache and darken my mood as well as my face

The face that smiles out of my phone screen is not me.

It doesn't show my shoes.

It doesn't show my triumphs and strengths.

My determination and wisdom.

It shows nothing of the beauty I had hoped would radiate forth

A result of managing the mind that is mine. I want to be a fighter.

Instead, it shows lines, dark circles, dyed hair to hide grey

Teeth in gums that are shot from five pregnancies

And a lifetime of bad things inflicted upon them

Under the pretence that not only was I in control of what they clamped on

But also that I knew what I was doing

Yet, the face that smiles out of my phone screen *is* me.

It shows my shoes.

It shows my triumphs and strengths.

My determination and wisdom.

It shows *all* of the beauty I had hoped would radiate forth

A result of managing the mind that is mine. I am a fighter.

It shows lines, dark circles, dyed hair to hide grey

Teeth in gums that are shot from five pregnancies

And a lifetime of bad things inflicted upon them

Under the pretence that not only was I in control of what they clamped on

But also that I knew what they were doing.

It shows my age.

I am that woman. Holder of Candles, Hands and Hearts.

2018

POETRY

I watched them come

And kneel by your side

With their regrets

Their memories

Their hot tears

Words they wished could be spoken

Desperate to see you again

And hold your hand

But you lay there,

Stone-faced and silent

Poetry is all they have of you now.

August 2019

MINE

I don't feel us getting old

I still look at you from across the room

Over the table

As you pass by my window on the way to fill up the car

And feel like no time has passed at all

Certainly not the twenty odd years that have!

Sure, I see the grey in your beard

My hands are not youthful anymore

The rings have dulled

But they're still a good fit as are you for me. I for you

Like no time has passed

Certainly, your father's words still ring in my ears

That we are too young to know what love is

And I told him. "Don't tell me!

You know me not. I am fifteen now!"

Aha! And so here we are.

A brick music box filled with echoes.

A tree full of family, all our very own.

Silvery etched lines.

Yours.

And mine.

2019

SUNDAY

Lazy, hazy

Cat stretched slumbers

Curtains whip the breeze

Tousled locks, unhurried sheets

As daylight comes to please.

Open, woken

Buttercups in

Amongst the lawn

Held beneath a willing chin

As golden as the dawn.

Scent, lent

To rainy drizzle

Bird song on the wing

Insists you lie a while longer

And breathe the morning in.

2019

PERSONAL TASTE

Oddly, I'm not partial

To a minty mouthed lover.

Fresh is far superior to extra strong anything.

Cigarettes laced with heat I could get used to. If I had to.

But I have never been a fan

Of kisses that taste only of gum.

I can think of much better ways to work a jaw.

And Lo! The two entwined!

Surely there is no worse fate

Than the taste of menthol masked smoke on bee stung lips.

Just saying.

2019

THIRTY EIGHT

Real, raw, wronged, righted, warrior, woman, mother, lover.

Writer, poet, fuck it, know it.

Post, the most.

Write, write, write, write.

Still awake. Dead of night.

Sing. See, that's the thing.

Workout, breastfeed, rock, sing.

Lather, wash, shit. Repeat.

Eat, drink, repeat. Sleep.

Thirty Eight.

2019

AUTUMN

I thought I heard her coming yesterday

Tickling the leaves

Shaking the laden fruit trees.

Blowing grey clouds into sugar whisps

Her work already begun.

This morning there's a chill about me

The suggestion of an extra blanket

Clothes airers and knitting

And I know she's here. Busy working.

2019

IF YOU SAY SO

Apparently, I'm getting old.

Apparently.

I'm so glad that someone noticed because Hot Dang! I had no idea!

Apparently, I'm detrimentally loyal and compassionate.

Apparently, that's a negative.

I don't always cook tea.

Sometimes I say "Eat your beans on toast and bloody Suck It Up."

Apparently, that just doesn't cut it.

Apparently, I don't run things the way the army would.

I'm more pirate.

There's swearing, drinking and a whole lot of dreaming of far off lands.

There's a treasure chest of loving too.

Wildness, character and rigging that reaches the stars!

Apparently, burning the candle at both ends is not a reason to ask for help.

Dark circles, empty breasts and insomnia go unnoticed.

But weakness and flaws, they get noticed.

Sometimes it's hard to see what's standing in front of you.

The same epically precious light that walks along side of you and also behind.

With fingers firmly hand-fasted to your shoulder.

Apparently, I'm lucky, not blessed.

Apparently.

2019

TIGHTLY WOUND

Seven years ago you put your bitchy little foot in my door.

There in some pretence that it was my responsibility

"Please Sir, can I have some..." More likely I never cared for you from the start.

Poor grip and kite strings slipped.

Panic! Ravaged? Rescued. Tick, tick, tick.

Not once but twice

Fate rolled the dice. Lady Luck?

By Fuck.

Next time 'twill be far too late.

43 carved on the gate.

2019

ALL SAINTS

November came heralding in this morning

The saints kept a quick step march behind

You were otherwise engaged and "busy"

So, sadly the sound never reached your eyes

2019

PART THREE

Beautiful Messy Life

39 to 41

Awake

ALL THE DAYS

I would look at you forever

Sleep with you for always

I would wake at 3am for all the days

So that you may hear my heart

Whispering "I love you."

2019

UNCONDITIONAL

Some days I feel like exhaustion is winning the battle

Sometimes I don't understand other people or their ways

Those days I grip the steering wheel and keep looking straight ahead

As the hot frustrated tears fall

Ignoring requests for the music to be turned up

Did I see the cow in the field? Are we nearly home yet?

Some days I take my plate and eat in the living room instead of at the table

I just want to taste my food

To eat without chewing around words of "stop, don't, quiet" and "no you may not"

Some days in my head

I plan we will share a movie or story all cosied up

But then I sneak off to my duvet, relieved I didn't voice the idea

I'm just too bone tired now.

But even on those days, I still want to know

About the one who feels sick and needs a bowl to take to bed

The one who came back in to say goodnight for the fifth time

The one who came in to say they couldn't cough but needed to

Even on those days, I still want to be the one

Who dashes to the stairs as I hear you stumble and fall

Ready to pick you up and check you over

I still want to be the one who holds you on my lap as you cry

Because you just didn't like the new vegan meal

Your sibling was mean and you have a sore throat

And you're sorry but you just want another hug

In the dead of the night on those days

I still want to be the one to rock you better through your fever

Even though I feel so worn.

There is nowhere I would rather be.

December 2019

GOD OF DOORS

You think you're the only one to be tired but you're not.

The only one to see reason for it all.

The plan. The direction. The goal.

You think yourself stronger. You're not.

We fight very different battles. Our days are worlds apart.

Neither one of us could fight so fiercely the others cause.

We are to walk together, for always.

Our paths parallel, each meandering across the others from time to time.

But January stokes the fire. Ends the last, begins the now.

Reflection being the most poignant word of the season.

A time for consideration.

Or time to see who stares back through the looking glass door.

January 2020

GRACE

I saw you on the path today

Walking alone down the road

Wondering where the little hand that used to hold onto yours had gone

I'm not sure you felt it

But I saw your shoulders drop

Lower than before

I saw you online today

Wondering why

Trying to make sense of the break in your heart

Why it couldn't work out the way you hoped

In spite of how hard you tried

How often you posted "happy pics"

The pretence let down by your eyes

I saw you on the bench today

Relieved to share

To talk about those hurtful words

That often taint your days

Glad it's not just you

Sense made

Of a nonsensical world

I saw you in the mirror today

I saw you falter at the injustice

As you came across an old photo

And cry a little in the kitchen

After the eyes rolled at soup for tea

The hand you held out, shunned

The plans you had, scarpered

Just before the selfie

Just before the post

I saw you change the track

Straighten your crown

And give yourself some grace

Today, you got through it

You are amazing

2020

SILENT NIGHT

For Brian Whittaker

This morn' had a little less birdsong.

My heart was a little less light.

The world feels a little less wonderful, now

That you have taken flight.

The noon had a little less ringing.

The sky seems a little less bright.

Conversation's a little less welcome right now,

Solace in Silent Night.

2020

THE ME YOU SEE

My lockdown?

Rediscovering through time that I am still the me I hope you see

Not just a wanna be

I was talking to my "voice of reason" yesterday

Getting all poetic and flowery

About how I'd never stopped being me over the years but I'd gotten hidden

My good old reason called me on it. In its own careful way.

The way it knows I need to be conversed with. Ha!

"Well! I am not the same." It said.

I conceded. Reflected. Retracted indeed!

No. Neither was I in truth. Yet, what did I mean?

Quite simply, I am.

I can. And I will.

The very kind of "am" I am to you, is your riddle to solve!

But I hope you like what you see.

July 2020

(Between March 2020 and March 2021, England encountered three national lockdowns to try to curb the spread of Covid-19. It was a global pandemic of Coronavirus disease.)

THIRTY NINE

What's the time?

39

38 hangs on the line

When it's dry, bring it in

Memories kept in biscuit tins

August 2020

TOMATO SOUP OR OTHER TINS

Today is a tomato soup for dinner day.

No roasts here.

Not even the offer of beans on toast!

No. Mama is not feeling the sudden busy culture, lockdown eased rush.

Tastes too much like stress & socially isolated loneliness to me.

Nope. Mama is here.

Her heart is here for you, her smile, her arms.

But not today the conversation.

Mama moves quietly today.

Tomorrow?

Sparkles and clockwork.

September 2020

(Between March 2020 and March 2021, England encountered three national lockdowns to try to curb the spread of Covid-19. It was a global pandemic of Coronavirus disease.)

SOMETIMES

Sometimes I take real good care of myself

I slather my face and body in frankincense

Burn oils, spend time with plants, eat raw vegan and work out

I even manage to drink water!

I listen to my mindfulness app at bedtime

Squeeze my pelvic floor and do a morning burst of yoga

Sometimes I take long walks

Knit and watch my children play on the rug

I listen to classical music, sing until my heart could burst

Recite beautiful prose to homeschoolers who dictate it

I bake cookies and Yorkshire puddings

I am there for them, him, you...

And then there are some times that I eat all the cake

I eat the pizza and the Halloween candy

And hide dark chocolate pieces in my hot milk

There are days and weeks that I put the scales in the bathroom I don't use.

I pretend I didn't used to need a belt to hold up my jeans.

My eyes feel treated because

I draw a black line around them for the first time in three weeks

My new birthday make-up lounges in its draw feeling dry and cakey

I promise myself I'm going to go to bed early

Lights out by 9:30 pm and at 1 am I'm squeezing

One. Last. Moment.

I hoover the crumbs off the table

Dust with baby wipes, make the 3-second rule stretch to 10

And eat my dinner last because there aren't enough clean forks

I serve dinner on toast or as soup.

I allow screens or prescribe early nights

I overthink the comment from my child's teacher

The look from the villager

There are days I am unsure what I will do tomorrow

To get through to bedtime

When I can rest and be still

And then I remember, it's all for a reason. And those reasons are everything

Sometimes it is super easy

Crystal clear and confident.

And sometimes it's everything else.

November 2020

NEVER MINE

If I could make you see what I see.

Make you feel, what I feel in my mother's heart.

If I could make you remember what it felt like to hold them

In your arms for the first time

And prepare you for the last time, so you would know it was coming.

You could bottle the moment.

If I could replay you,

Your promises to be the best you could be. That you'd always be there for them.

No matter what.

If I could play you,

The first time they laughed. The first time they called your name.

If I could make you see the world through my heart

Would you truly begin to understand how as I grew them, they are me?

Each and every one.

And that when they see the world their way, I see myself teetering on a ledge, wearing their shoes.

If I could make you understand

Why I grow quiet when I watch them all play.

When simple untarnished words and worlds don't exist

And instead all there is, is excitement and thrill.

A simple snowfall transporting them back to the days I can't let go of.

If I could make you see,

No, really see,

How their baby cheeks are fading as quick as the sand you try to hold in your hands,

Would you finally take a load off?

Just sit all laid back on your chair and smile.

So, whenever they turned their glance towards you, that is all they would ever see?

If I could show you, me at 3 am silently worrying in the dark.

If I could make you see that you will one day do the same.

Praying to Gods you didn't know you cared for,

To "Please, let me have done enough".

Enough that they know, without a moment's hesitation,

That you are there and that they can always come home.

Where they can feel safe.

If I could make you understand the reason why I never told you,

I had to pull the car over just the other day.

The pain became too much and started leaking from my eyes

Because I realised...

We will always be theirs

But they were never ours.

January 2021

SMALL YET MIGHTY

I spilt my tea today

A takeaway cup balanced precariously as I held the door for another

En route to a ballet lesson.

Before I'd even taken a sip

And I wanted to cry

Great, fat, ugly sobs to add to the puddle

"My poor tea!" I wanted to wail, but really I was sorry for myself

Because it's not the tea is it?

It's what the tea represents

How the ritual helps me to ride the waves of the most difficult parts of my day

A much better friend than that bitch the wine witch who only ever took away.

It's a hug when I'm lonely. Not alone. Lonely

An "I love you" from me to me, when there's no one else to tell me

Comforting when I'm trying really hard or when something's not working

A "Come on then gel*, deep breath"

A "you've got this"

An "it's going to be ok"

A "nevermind"

The one little bit of me time and self-care I can almost rely on showing up

Even if it does go cold.

June 2021

AWOL

It's on its way but seems to be held up somewhere,

The miracle of womanhood we were blessed to be born with.

Every month the same feelings as our younger sisters

But not yet sleeping the in the same sweaty sheets as our elder ones.

The same frustrated hot tears, the same uncomfortable jeans,

The same ill-fitting overstretched bra, suddenly filled with tender, weighted breasts.

Nothing to show for a month of courageous navigating.

The dog's having a field day with your empty chocolate wrappers,

As you stuff in yet another pain au chocolat and hug your hot water bottle tighter.

You're not even really sure where it went.

Normally the screw opens the bottle but you suppose the wine is corked.

Damp, stained and snapped in half. The last bit clogging up the neck.

Fuck.

Sometimes you think your dear old aunt is actually going to make an appearance after all.

The tissue's pink where she blotted her lipstick.

But then you remember an overzealous visitor of another kind.

Still a welcome one but, not quite the same.

The reason you want to go to the show so bad is precisely because

You know one day the travellers will hit the road.

You'll be standing there in your pretty white dress

With flowers in your hair and crow's feet by your eyes,

Wondering why you weren't allowed to come before.

The empty canvas sheet flailing wildly as it breaks free several tent pegs.

It's just you, the crickets and the ringmaster's face on the circus poster.

And someone's drawn on a beard and glasses, so you can't take him seriously.

It's not that you need it now.

The days of bubbling, babies belonging to you, long passed.

It's not that you are afraid of the day your last egg slips calmly and unceremoniously from your womb.

It's the fixed race.

The doctor leaning back in his brown leather chair,

In the small office in the back of your mind.

Fingers drumming together with an air of impatience.

"You are done, but you are *not* done, my dear.

Until one day you are!

It's all so much less messy, you see?"

And I do see.

But I still don't like it.

January 2022

I DO

Do you know why it is

That after such impatient anticipation

A new mother cries desolate after birth

And clutches her shrivelled paunch?

I do.

I know what it is to feel

My breath catch in my eyes

Tears spring from my heart

To hear a womb wail as she mourns the parting

I do.

We had no notion that it would be

The only part of their journey

We could truly hold them

The shortest path

Do I forgive you for saying you wish you could eat your baby?

I do.

And childhood's ride is just as short

Where all a mother's youth gets spent

Sticky lips & fingers need wiping less & less

I rely on dreams now

To remind me of that sweet weight on my knee

The head lolling on my shoulder

Daylight blurs my palm somewhat

Where their hand used to fit

It's a fearsome place

Our side of the clock face

And I know why

I do.

January 2022

TIME-STAND-STILL

And I will sing to your heart

The Time-Stand-Still place where we never part

Night time snuggles in the dark

Saying the first of many goodbyes.

I still remember the first time

Still remember the last sign

That reminded me, you never were mine

But I am yours.

The first days my arms encircled and

Tied each ribbon loose by the thousand

The hours spent spinning them by hand

I never once made enough.

They do talk about the pain

Of breastfeeding and moan about the rain

Deflated bosoms, never quite the same

Seldom cherry bud lips stuck fast.

The real pain of the first cuts

Those darling ribbons, one or two, not much!

Off my knee and into such and such

The last feed. Goodbye, my love.

Hot bath sees my heart break

Life-giving milk floats out, my breasts ache

Such a waste, tears flow, for fuck sake

No "one last time" ever long enough.

No photo warm enough to please

No sleepy cheek, no gentle squeeze

No sharp head turns or bitey teeth!

Three years forgot, latch lost.

And so I write you poems of love

As we dance and turn full circle 'cause

Those last ribbons reach in front, above

Behind, aside, no more.

And I will forever hold your heart

In Time-Stand-Still place, we never part

Where I began and you did start

Where goodbyes never find us.

2022

MAKING GOOD

With day break, mist lifts.

Worries set sail eventide.

Plates can spin again.

2022

ROSIE LEE

As always she talks me through the storm.

Reliable as ever. Lightens and sweetens each salty teardrop.

She takes my hands and warms them. Kisses my lips and the corners of my mouth, until the faintest of smiles appears.

Her eyes darken like melted chocolate.

Not that I believe it of any use.

The Bow bells ring.

My head throbs. I'm in no mood for the party, I tell her. Tears brim hot and spicy once more and spill over without permission.

"Shhh, it's ok. I know exactly what you need." She assures me.

Gently, she strokes my brow. "Thankyou," I whisper as I gaze into her. She stirs so leisurely.

I feel her strength pour into me. My eyelashes flutter open to her hoop earrings, twinkling below her headscarf.

Her scent catches my skin

as she reaches across me and fumbles for the bees and honey.

She hesitates at the door.

"You're going to do great things," she says. And I love her.

She may not be everybody's but she's mine.

2022

FAILED AT THAT

It's been bad.

Not as bad as it could be

Not as sad as it could be

But bad all the same.

A crap day.

A very flat day

A "I wish I had a mum day"

But there's no one up for the job

And I'm not hiring.

It's been one of those

"Where's my fucking fags?" days

"I'm just gonna buy a pack" days

But they don't do tens no more

And I don't smoke.

I've had a right

"God give me strength" day

"For God sake someone take me away" day

But there's too much noise to hear a reply

And I'm sick of listening.

I just fancy it being

A "Come day, go day"

A wine o clock day

A Gin from the shop day

A Vodka and pop day

But I don't drink.

Tomorrow is a new day.

So they say

I'm all for betting it'll be a good day

But I don't...

2022

AUSPICIOUS HAPPENSTANCE

You sought me today,

In the kitchen,

And just for a fraction,

We stepped off the merry-go-round.

All there was to be seen,

All that mattered,

Was you in my arms.

And it struck me right there,

Between the ribs,

And took with it my breath,

Just how beautiful you are.

An achingly precious happening,

To have you to hold,

How blessed am I that you love me too?

And as I stare in wonder,

I see you twenty years from now,

Simply glowing. Utterly breathtaking.

Striding forward, your kind heart,

Pouring love into everyone you meet.

Yet still, you free yourself,

Bound off to play.

Leaving me with the feeling,

I've arrived at the bottom of the escalator.

All a-daze.

As the world around me,

Resumes its rushing.

2022

LITTLE GREEN LIGHT

I see your little green light.

Heralding that yes indeed,

You are there and will be for a long time.

But, confirming that I could not be further from your thoughts.

2022

DIRTBAG

I didn't choose to love you

When I found you in my urine on a stick

I didn't know I'd love you

I hoped I would

The rest is sixteen years of history

Oh, I know you didn't ask for it

But, you don't get to tell me not to bother

I won't return you either

2022

SHELL ISLAND

Today we went a-hunting,

For shells upon the sand.

We took a line for crabbing,

A bucket in my hand.

We slipped and slid down sand dunes,

Caught cockles in the sea.

We walked along the river,

My little one and me.

We camped and had a fire,

Watched the soft sun set.

Listened to the rain all night,

The canvas getting wet.

And everywhere that I went,

You ran on just ahead,

Smiling and waving back,

"A big boy now" you said.

Today we went a-hunting,

For shells upon the sand.

You were everywhere and nowhere,

To swing between our hands.

2022

(Shell Island is a special place in Wales. We used to go there to camp before we had children and since have taken all of them with us. This year our two youngest went for the first time but our eldest stayed home. It was sad).

MABON

Autumn tugs my sleeve

"Slow down."

"Not quite yet" the broom beckons

"Still much to do."

But the eiderdown has other ideas

And the new cold, under my feet when I alight in the morning.

September 2022

MUM GUILT

They get angry when I'm busy
And I feel guilty every time
They throw me disappointed looks
For making some time mine

They have me question often
If it's me that fails to see
Should I always stop when they demand
To spend some time with me?

There's no such thing as balance
In Motherhood, you won't
Succeed in pleasing everyone
Damned if you do or don't.

2022

EPIPHANY

January tentatively puts a tip toe through the door

Worried he's nothing good to offer, can't be sure

Yule takes such a lot of thunder, hogs the floor

Bleakest of bleak midwinters, no chance of thaw

But January bangs a blinding brilliance, sky puts on a show

Jack plays with frosty kisses, ignites wanton sparkles in the snow

January's heart burns such a glory, all day keeps wicks a-glow

And with his icy breath, he whispers "Would you like to come and know?"

January makes a welcome table, keeps a warm fire in the hearth

For the weary, lost and hopeful who slip and slide upon his path

Full of promise holds the lantern, hot pennies placed upon the glass

Roast crab apples, toasting cider, Wassailer's know he soon shall pass

2022

INTRUDER

On the day you were born, as I lay there exhausted

Vowing to protect you forever, the uninvited visitor came in.

They slipped through the door, climbed in at my side

And whispered so softly, in a sweet angelic voice

"But, what if you die?"

At first, I thought they meant you, and I was terrified.

I held you tighter, and never deeply slept again, ever.

I would watch you want to do things and I would have to let you,

But all the time I was there just behind

To catch you should you fall. And die.

I would do things, so many things with you.

I would take so many pictures! How happy you made us.

I'd shower you with my kisses until you would run away.

But I needed to make sure you'd gotten enough.

In case you died.

One night when you were five, there was an intruder in the house.

I heard them slide their hand along the wall,

As they felt their way up the stairs in the dark.

I could hear them standing at the top deciding which room to go into.

My mind raced with terror once more. In case they hurt you. And you died.

But instead, they came into my room and I knew then, who it was.

The same old, creaking body. The same lifeless, brittle, grey hair.

The same foul smelling, rotting smile.

Once more, they climbed in at my side and with their oh-so-soft

Sweet angelic voice they whispered, "What if you die?"

And I finally understood. I lay there unable to take a breath.

The sheer magnitude of its meaning rendered me an almighty blow

I'd been wasting so much time! How could I have been so naive

To think myself incapable of hurting you? How would I ever prepare you?

What

    If

        I

           Die?

2022

FROM THE ARCHIVES

Where it Began

Teen to Twenties

Feeling

(Here I have included a small selection of my very earliest poetic work. Whilst it was never to be my best, I am often reminded when I read it that, even in youth there can be great passion.
As the saying goes "Still Waters Run Deep").

TEENAGE GIRL IN LOVE

You know that certain boy?

And that word, Love?

Well, when do you know,

If it happened to you?

And how can you tell?

Is it Love when

You know his star sign,

His favourite food,

His pet hate?

You dream about him,

Can't stop thinking about him,

Race to the phone, just in case it's him,

Cry & mope when it isn't him,

Miss him when you're away from him,

You're on top of the world when you're with him,

Blush every time you see him?

Is it Love when

You overspill with delight when he smiles,

Go green with envy when it's at someone else?

Get all excited when you arrange to go out with him,

Feel all tingly when you kiss him,

Constantly talk about him,

You just can't stop thinking about him.

But is it Love when, something inside,

Still feels unsure & a little insecure?

But unsure of what?

And how come you feel like crying?

1995

BLIZZARD

Sharp stones fall from above,

Arms wave & thrash in the wind.

Splinters of glass blow about,

As I watch safe from behind my window.

1995

TRAPPED

Like a rabbit in a snare,

A fox on the run,

A pheasant flying high,

From the poacher's gun.

Like a slave in shackles,

A prisoner in the cell,

No one to talk to,

No one to tell.

Like a flame reaching out,

For someone to tend,

The wicks burning thin,

It's nearing its end.

Like the mother & the child,

Screaming for attention,

Like something's going on,

That no one's to mention.

Like the caller on the phone,

Who doesn't want to tell,

The undertaker's grinning,

A heart that has fell.

Like a ferret down a rabbit hole,

A scream then it's gone,

An opera singer singing,

But there isn't any song.

Like the star that has fallen,

Someone has died,

There's no where to run,

And no where to hide.

1996

INFLICTION

But it's so hard to swallow,

The lump of emotion,

Locked in place at the back of your throat.

And the bone of hurt is still stuck in my teeth,

Escapism descends,

Reality hits hard.

The needle of suspicion,

Pierces the back of my throat,

It punctures my skin once so supple.

And the lines on my forehead reach out like branches,

Showing every worry I ever had.

I choke on confusion & deny all existence.

Every breath that I take,

Pricks my conscience like pins,

I suffocate & writhe in depression.

And though all in vain,

I search for the key,

You blow out the light,

A sickly sweet incense engulfs the air.

Innocence & virginity,

Whisper the past,

Offering a chance to find warmth.

But you twist the knife & rub in the pain,

My heart beats its last,

Life is destroyed as you pull the plug.

1997

APPRECIATIVE LOVER

You say you love me,

Then say it and mean it.

If you don't,

Don't say it all.

You want to make love to me,

Then feel and touch me.

Kiss & caress

All of me, nothing less.

Care for me, show me, support me,

Secure me tight in your arms.

Think what a precious you have in your life,

Someone who's there for you,

Loves, helps and cares for you.

Please never again hurt my feelings,

I need you, be there and be mine.

I give and you take, so stir and awake,

For you might need me too sometime.

1999

BEAST

Deep within the folds of trees,

He crouches low amongst the leaves.

Their sugar frosted patterns glisten,

He holds his breath, ears pricked to listen.

The full moon slumbers way up high,

Casting shadows in his eyes,

Breathing deep, one foot poised,

Careful not to make a noise.

Slow and curling breath expels,

His chest silently heaves and swells,

Stealthily creeping across the ground,

Leaving footprints all around.

Glancing back across his shoulder,

Wisdom came as he got older,

No place here for small and weak,

The lifeless creature clamped in his teeth.

A sharp crack sounds from behind,

But it's too late to change his mind,

It's now or never, fear starts to creep,

One last look and then...he leaps!

2007

ABOUT THE AUTHOR

Juliette Proffitt is an author and poet who decided in her fortieth year to fulfill a childhood dream and finally self publish her work!

She writes with a relatable and reassuring, conversational tone that leaves her readers and followers feeling like she has all the time in the world, just for them.

Juliette was born in Leicestershire in 1981 and was an only child.

As a young girl, she was not very academic or artistic instead, her talents were to be found in reading, writing and singing. She spent a great deal of time making up stories of her own or singing Beatles songs on the garden wall and reenacting comedy sketches of the Golden Girls with her cousins!

At the tender age of fifteen, she met her now partner, Ian. After several years they bought their family home and got engaged. Together they have six beautiful children and a wonderful Kerry Blue Terrier, named Dani.

Juliette is proud to be able to be a full time, stay-at-home, home educating parent.

In 2017 all of her children were given the opportunity to be home educated. Over time her eldest three children entered secondary school education but she still home educates her three youngest to this day and their journey can be followed on Instagram and Facebook at Beautiful Messy Life.

Printed in Great Britain
by Amazon

19665077R00108